Anti-Paraclete

by

W.B. Godbey

First Fruits Press
Wilmore,
Kentucky
c2018

Anti-paraclete.
By W.B. Godbey.
First Fruits Press, © 2018

ISBN: 9781621718062 (print), 9781621718079 (digital), 9781621718086 (kindle)

Digital version at http://place.asburyseminary.edu/godbey/15/

Godbey, W. B. (William Baxter), 1833-1920.

Anti-Paraclete / W.B. Godbey. – Wilmore, KY : First Fruits Press, ©2018.
pages 36; cm 21.

Reprint. Previously published: Cincinnati, Ohio : God's Revivalist Office, [190-?]

Contents: Anti-Paraclete -- 1. Personality of the Paraclete -- 2. The unpardonable sin -- 3. How do we commit the unpardonable sin? -- 4. Beware of counterfeits.

ISBN: 9781621718062 (paperback)

1. Holy Spirit. 2. Sin, Unpardonable. I. Title.

BT122.G62 2018   231.3

Cover design by John Ramsay

asburyseminary.edu
800.2ASBURY
204 North Lexington Avenue
Wilmore, Kentucky 40390

First Fruits
THE ACADEMIC OPEN PRESS OF ASBURY SEMINARY

First Fruits Press
The Academic Open Press of Asbury Theological Seminary
204 N. Lexington Ave., Wilmore, KY 40390
859-858-2236
first.fruits@asburyseminary.edu
asbury.to/firstfruits

Anti-paraclete

W. B. GODBEY

Published for the Author
by
GOD'S REVIVALIST PRESS
Cincinnati, Ohio

ANTI-PARACLETE.

"Paraclete" is a compound of two Greek words, *kletos,* a participle, from the verb *kaleo,* to call, and the preposition *para,* which means, "by your side." In the New Testament this significant Greek compound is applied to the Holy Ghost in the capacity of Comforter, as He is the Executive of the Trinity, the Convicter or the sinner, the Regenerator of the penitent, the Sanctifier of the believer, the Restorer of the backslider, and the Glorifier of the pilgrim when this mortal shall put on immortality.

The prepositional prefix of the word used as the cognomen of this book, means "instead of." Therefore the anti-paraclete is a person who takes the place of the Holy Ghost in the capacity of the Christian's Comforter. You will be surprised to hear of anyone having done such a thing, as it is audacity transcendently diabolical, such that I could hardly believe it till I came in contact with it.

I have preached more in Los Angeles, Cal., than in any other place in all this world, as I always make it my headquarters when I visit Southern California. No wonder it has a mongrel population of all nationalities, because its magnetism draws on every point of the compass.

The Holiness Movement is stronger there than elsewhere in all the earth, the city abounding in churches and missions heroically pressing the battle for God and holiness, in this genial and lovely clime. It is axiomatic that when God works the devil never fails to do his utmost to counterfeit all the good and defeat every enterprise of heavenly philanthropy. Consequently Los Angeles is the hotbed of heresies.

The Tongue Movement, which has so awfully damaged the kingdom of God, as it runs His noble saints into demonism and gets them so tangled up and bewildered that few, I fear, ever make their escape, was launched in the "City of the Angels." At that time I was preaching in New York City, when God sent one of His prophets with an especial message calling me to Los Angeles. Having crossed, the continent, on arrival I find the city on tiptoe, and the "Gift of Tongues" all the go; people out at all the depots, meeting the trains at all hours of the day and night, as the Holiness people were coming from the ends of the earth to satisfy their curiosity and to get their souls blessed.

I enjoyed the favor of the leader, Rev. Seymour (colored), from Dixie Land, who claimed the honor of pioneering the movement in the city. The meeting was running night and day without intermission. All pilgrims were met by an expectant friend and escorted to the Tongue meeting; your humble servant enjoying the service of the leader.

On arrival, they at once propounded the question, "Have you received the baptism of the Holy Ghost?" to which the pilgrim responded in the affirmative. Then they said, "Have you received the sign?" The answer came back, "What sign?" The response followed, "Speaking with tongues," Then the negative answer proclaimed a candidacy for the altar, at which the seeker fell and where he stayed night and day, till they got him hypnotized, mesmerized, and demonized, so that he rose with ejaculatory, ecstatic utterances, understood by no one. The solution is found in the simple fact that the air is thronged with demons. (Eph. 2:2.) We are nowhere commanded to seek anything but the Lord, as the Word so beautifully rings in our ears: "Seek ye the Lord while he may be found; call ye upon him while he is near; let the wicked man forsake his way and the unrighteous man his thoughts, let him return unto the Lord who will have mercy on him, and to our God who will abundantly pardon." When you seek anything but God, an evil spirit at once comes in and gives you something in order to get you away from Him. If they could give you a language, they would certainly do it, but they cannot. I know languages which you do not know, but I could not give you one to save my life.

The magicians, sorcerers, necromancers, jugglers, wizards, witches, Spiritualists and Mormons in all ages have had this so-called "Gift of Tongues," which is really no tongue, because tongue (*"glossa"*) has no meaning but language, and it is a well-demonstrated fact that they have no tongue, but these noises like birds and frogs, imparted by evil spirits.

The gift of tongues is all right. I wrote a book twenty years ago which the Lord has wonderfully used, "Spiritual Gifts and Graces," showing up the nine graces by which we are saved, love, joy, peace, long-suffering, kindness, goodness, meekness, faith and holiness; and the nine gifts by which we help save others (I Cor. 12:8-11), wisdom, knowledge, faith, bodily healing, the manipulations of dynamites, prophecy, discernment of spirits, tongues and the interpretation of tongues.

They received the gift of tongues at Pentecost, and at other times in the Apostolic Age and many receive it now, to my personal knowledge.

When I came to their meeting in Los Angeles they asked me if I had received the baptism of the Holy Ghost, to which I responded in the affirmative. Then they asked me if I had the sign, "speaking with tongues." I suppose I was the first one among the hundreds and thousands who had arrived and been thus interviewed, to give them an affirmative answer, "I thank God I can say with Paul, 'I speak with tongues more than you all'" proceeding unhesitatingly to do so.

CHAPTER I.

It is to be regretted that somebody in bygone ages got an "o" in place of an "e" in this word *ghest,* which means a precious friend, coming not simply to make you a transient visit, but to abide with you and help you in your labors of love, cooperate with you in prayer and faith, patience, and all your philanthropic enterprises. Just as my good old friend, James L. Hunton, at Orange, Cal., whom God has blessed not only with salvation, but a princely fortune. Every time he sees me, he begs me to take my good old wife and come to his house of many mansions, select rooms, and be at home the remnant of our days, at the same time charging me to bring no money, assuring me that every bill is paid till the trumpet blows. He says he just wants us for company in life's evening, *i. e.,* that we should be his guests.

Rest assured we are living in the last days, when we need not be surprised at anything. As Los Angeles is the Jerusalem of the New World, the focalization of God's holy people, it is also the hotbed of heresies, and it seems that when anyone gets ready to launch some newfangled, unheard-of, Hell-hatched heresy, he makes for Los Angeles. So here we find a man claiming to be the Comforter Himself.

How strange to think any man would ever take the place of the Holy Ghost, absolutely usurp His office and not only claim it, but openly repudiate His personality; and then still more paradoxical, that such an one would have a following, especially when we contemplate God's Word appertaining to the blessed Trinity and human duty and responsibility. There are not three gods, as we might vainly conclude, and actually we are in danger of trending into the tri-theistical heresy, which is reached by the unwarranted differentiation of the three persons of the Godhead.

The Father sits upon the throne of the universe, while countless millions of rolling worlds, each accompanying his own magnitudinous solar orb, move in their diversified systems around His effulgent throne, responsive to His omnific *ipse dixit*. Meanwhile the Son sits upon the mediatorial throne at His side and intercedes for this lost world. N. B. The Holy Ghost is the Spirit of the Father (Acts 5:3, 4 and 9,) whom He sends into this lost world to convict the sinner, convert the penitent, reclaim the backslider, sanctify the believer, and glorify the disembodied pilgrim when this mortal puts on immortality.

Therefore, when the loving Father saves a soul on this holy mountain ("Mt. of Blessings," Cincinnati, Ohio), He executes the work through His omnipotent Agent, the Holy Ghost.

We also have the clear revelation appertaining to the Son of God, *i. e.,* the synonymy of the Holy Ghost (Acts 16:6-7). When Paul, Timothy, Silas and Luke were pushing the evangelistic work in Galatia, Pamphylia and other states in southwestern Asia, verse six says Paul was forbidden to preach the Word in Asia; for God wanted him at that time to carry the Gospel into Europe, the very thing for us, as we are all Europeans. Led by the Spirit, they were all traveling toward the northwest, confronted by the greatest sea in the world, not far away. Therefore when they reach Mysia, which borders on the sea, they were "endeavoring to go into Bithynia," lying eastward and giving them the great continent, four thousand miles of *terra firma,* for evangelistic work.

If he had followed his own mind, he would have gone, but he dared not disobey the Holy Ghost. Consequently he entered Mysia and went right down to Troas on the sea. N. B.—The arts of navigation were in their infancy, and the mariner's compass and the steam engine never dreamed of. During the ensuing night the Lord clears up all this bewilderment by the vision of a Macedonian, far beyond the sea, standing and shouting aloud, "Come over into Macedonia and help us!"

N. B.—Verse six said he was forbidden by the Holy Ghost, and seven that when his human mind led him toward Bithynia, the Spirit of Jesus did not permit him. Mark this notable fact, *i. e.,* the synonymy of the Holy Ghost in verse six and the

Spirit of Jesus in verse seven; thus revealing clearly the identity of Jesus and the Holy Spirit. As in Chapter Five we have already seen the identity of the Father and the Holy Spirit, hence the unity of the Divinity, and the legitimate conclusion that there is but one God, who does His great, glorious, beneficent and philanthropic work in three distinct personalities, accommodatory to our finite senses in the comprehension of the wonderful plan of salvation.

CHAPTER II

Our Savior tells us (Matt. 12:31,32) that the sin against the Father shall be forgiven, and the same is true of the sin against the Son, but the blasphemy of the Spirit is never forgiven, either in this age or that which is to come. ("World," in the English version, leads you astray, and encourages the Hell-redemption heresy, involving the implication that there will be a chance for lost souls in the world to come. This simple correction and the use of the word "age" perfectly relieves the difficulty.) You see our Savior positively certifies that the blasphemy of the Spirit is never forgiven, either in the present age, or the oncoming Millennium, now dawning and collapsing on the Gentile dispensation.

Now let us diagnose the gracious economy of the redemptive scheme. You see the Father sits upon the throne of the universe, and the Son by His side. Whereas the Father convicts sinners, converts penitents, reclaims backsliders, sanctifies believers, and glorifies disembodied pilgrims through the medium of His Holy Spirit, whom He freely and unstintedly pours out on all appreciative hearts. In a similar manner our loving Savior, now in His glory, inter-

11

ceding for this lost world, freely sends His Holy
Spirit and executes His mighty works through His
instrumentality, having actually assured us in that
wonderful and beautiful prayer He has given us
(Luke 11:13), "If ye being evil know how to give
good gifts unto your children, how much more will
your Father who is from heaven give his Holy Spirit
to them that ask him?"

Therefore you see we have every conceivable en-
couragement to ask the loving Father, as well as our
blessed interceding Savior, to give us the Holy Spirit.

This world is full of penniless beggars. There
is a great eleemosynary institution inexhaustibly supplied with everything they need and delighted to
lavish it out in superabounding munificence. Here
is a man utterly destitute, winter coming on and
no protection from the blizzards and nothing to eat.
Now this grand philanthropy is managed by three
officers, the one in London, the world's metropolis;
another in New York, the Columbian metropolis;
but the third officer is everywhere on the face of the
whole world at the same time. This shivering, starv-
ing pauper refuses to receive the benefaction from
the man here in Cincinnati, but says, "I want the
man in London." Now he has not a penny to defray
his traveling expenses, he cannot get to London, so
he must take it from the man in Cincinnati or he
will inevitably perish right here. Another says, "I
will not receive the needed pabulum and clothing
from the man in the Queen City, but I will take
the one in New York." It takes $15 to run to New

York, and he has not a solitary penny; therefore in Cincinnati he must die a pauper. This illustration applies to every human being, as the storehouse is absolutely inexhaustible and the 1,700 millions of people now on the earth have nothing to do but avail themselves of an irrefragible thesaurus, at their option, and nothing to do but check on it for all they want, and the larger the check the better the Heavenly Teller is pleased and the more brilliantly He smiles. "Why did you not check for more?"

N. B.—The Holy Ghost is none other than very and eternal God, omnipresent, knocking at the door of every human pauper in all the world. Jesus says the blasphemy of the Spirit is never forgiven, either in this age or the future. When I was a little boy, studying old Dillingworth's spelling book, I remember this sentence, "Blasphemy is contemptuous treatment of God," which simply means that you utterly ignore Him, and will not have Him, actually insulting Him, saying to Him, "Go Thy way; attend to Your own business. I do not need You."

There is a law in our country called "the contempt of court." In countless instances, people would do almost anything to avoid going into court and testifying in a pending case; actually leaving the country and hiding away in the jungles of the antipodean world, to avoid giving a testimony that would tie the rope around the neck.

God is not only loving and lovely, but He is Love itself (I John 4:8, 16), and Love cannot keep from loving. He so loved the world "that he gave his only begotten Son, that whosoever believeth in him should not perish, but have eternal life." (John 3:16.) Ransack the classical ages and nations, from Moses, one of the first of ancient writers, down to the present day, flooded with literature, poetry, oratory, philosophy, every ramification of science and profoundest erudition; call up all the lexicographers ever produced, by Greece, Rome, Germany, England, and America, and ask them to fathom the depth, soar to the altitude, broaden into the latitude, press forward into the longitude of that little adverb "so" in that wonderful Scripture, which defines how much God loved the world. The brilliant procession of the world's lexicographers turn pale and retreat, confessing their utter incompetency for the emergency.

> "Oh, for this love, let rocks and hills,
>   Their lasting silence break,
> And all harmonious human tongues
>   Their Savior's praises speak.
> Angels, assist our mighty joys,
>   Strike all your harps of gold;
> But when you reach your highest notes
>   This love can ne'er be told."

Such is the superabounding love of God that no soul ever goes down to Hell unless he takes the bit in his teeth, runs away with the salvation wagon, and precipitates it over a precipice till it is dashed into smithereens, his hopeless soul taking the awful plunge into a bottomless Hell. In my voyages across the great oceans, I have often been awakened in the dead hours of the long, dreary night by the reports of the sounders, giving the depth of the sea, in their strange nautical language, till finally the stentorian roar salutes my ears reminding me of Gabriel's trumpet blast, "No bottom!" meaning that the sea is too deep to be sounded by lead and line, but reminding me of the mournful wails of the damned in Hell, through the rolling centuries, ages and cycles, roaring out "No bottom!" sinking into a deeper damnation, the fiery billows rolling over them in consuming floods of unquenchable flame and still "no bottom," deeper down and more awful hell, but yet, "no bottom."

The Holy Ghost is the Executive of the Trinity, whose glorious philanthropic office, in His normal and indefatigable and unutterable loving kindness and tender mercies is to convict every sinner, convert every penitent, restore every backslider, and sanctify every believer; yet it is optional with the people to let Him do His work, as God never saves anybody against his will. In so doing, He would dehumanize you, so you would never be a man any more. You might be a raccoon, a kangaroo, or an ourang-outang, but never a man, as perfect freedom is inseparable from humanity. Therefore, when we do not reciprocate the beneficent offices of the Holy Ghost, we are treating Him with contempt, grieving Him away, and sealing our doom in endless woe.

CHAPTER III.

How Do We Commit the Unpardonable Sin?

We are liable to commit the blasphemy of the Holy Ghost in many ways, thus crossing the dead line, and sealing our doom for endless woe. This great salient fact of the unpardonable sin against the Holy Ghost, Jesus pronounces "blasphemy," which simply means treating Him with contempt, ignoring His great and glorious work in the execution of the redemptive scheme.

As the redeeming grace of God in Christ normally reaches every soul, in the prenatal state, antecedently to the physical birth (Heb. 2:9: That "by the grace of God He tasted death for every one"), therefore the moment soul and body united, constitute personality, the grace of God in Christ supervenes; justification is sealed in Heaven, without faith or works, but for Christ's sake alone, and the Holy Spirit instantaneously creates the Divine life in that mortal spirit, responsively to His executive office in the new creation.

Therefore by the wonderful grace of God in Christ, every human being is born in the Kingdom, justified and regenerated; not born sinners, as Calvinism teaches, but sinful, *i. e.*, full of inbred sin by

heredity which is quickly manifested, by evil pas-
sions cropping out. Yet inbred sin does not un-
Christianize them any more than adult Christians,
who are not sanctified and so full of inbred sin, are
un-Christianized. The prodigal son and his father
abundantly confirm the conclusion that, through the
wonderful atonement Jesus made on rugged Calvary,
every human being is born a Christian. Oh! what
a glorious run Jesus made on the devil, who had
achieved the greatest victory of the ages in Eden
when he captured Adam, because every human being
was in him, and all died when he sinned. (First
Corinthians 15:22: "In Adam all die, so truly in
Christ shall all be made alive.")

When does this revivification in Christ supervene?
Why, the very moment you become a human being,
by the union if soul and body. Therefore the spiritual birth precedes the physical, which seems flatly
contradicted in John 3:3, "born again," which would
put the spiritual birth after the physical, and send
to Hell every child that ever died antecedently to
the physical birth, awful to contemplate, as it would
fill up Hell with unborn infants.

This shows the great importance of having the
correct Scripture. "Born again" is preached and
sung and testified throughout Christendom, at the
same time involving the awful heresy of infantile
damnation. Jesus never said "born again." The
Greek *palin* means again, and is not in this pass-
age; but *anothen,* which simply means "from

above." Oh! how important to know the correct
Scripture, so that we will preach, testify and sing
"born from above." The new life comes down from
Heaven when the Holy Ghost, who is always in
Heaven even while on earth, creates it in the dead
soul.

Therefore every human being is born a Christian,
but full of depravity. (Psalms 51:5: "I was shapen
in iniquity, and in sin did my mother conceive me.")
Campbellites, who are Pelagians, and do not believe
in depravity, do their best to vitiate that Scripture,
identifying it with David's mother alone;—utterly
untenable. Peter says, "No Scripture is of private
interpretation," confirming the conclusion that *all*
Scripture applies to the *whole* human race, and consequently the blessed Bible is literally and actually
every man's biography.

All infants are Christians, as Jesus abundantly
confirms by His preaching, certifying over and over,
"Of such is the kingdom of heaven," and holding them
up as paragon members, assuring adult sinners that,
unless they get converted and become as little children, they cannot enter the Kingdom. While felic-
itously all the human race are born justified and regenerated, *bona fide* citizens of the Kingdom, yet
that innate depravity superinduces the absolute
necessity of conversion, because it turns the face
away from God, toward this wicked world, so, if
nothing is done, we sadly all verify that terrific
Scripture, "Infants go away as soon as they are born,
speaking lies." "We are prone to do evil as the

sparks to go upward," the depravity, hereditary in every heart, superinducing that proneness.

Conversion simply means turning around. God's time for conversion is in infancy, antecedently to the forfeiture of our innate justification, which we can only do by committing known sin after we reach accountability. If God had His way, there would not be a sinner on the earth living under condemnation, with Satan's black lasso round his neck, and ready every moment to drop into Hell. Our glorious Christ has so wonderfully and triumphantly redeemed the world as to preclude the necessity of a solitary damnation.

The Holy Ghost is the Spirit of Christ, who shines on every human spirit coming into the world. (John 1:9.) He calls every one in infancy, as in case of your humble servant, whom He blessedly called to salvation and the Gospel ministry through the instrumentality of his sainted mother, before she took off the baby clothes. I know not how old I was, but I do know my grandfather had come to see me, and brought me a dress, because I was named for him, and I had it on (girl fashion). Mother preached to me the everlasting Gospel with the Holy Ghost sent down from Heaven, and I drank it in deliciously, got converted and called to preach, and never afterward doubted it, either. That is the reason why I am so abundant in labor, preaching these sixty-one years, and this being the 137th book of my authorship, every one telling the reader the sure way to Heaven. I owe this superabounding labor for the

Lord to my infantile conversion, which fortified me against Satan's black lasso and kept me from running away and sowing wild oats, as most people do, and multiplied millions go down to Hell to reap them. I know not the taste of any of the intoxicating drinks, never tasted beer, nor used tobacco, nor knew the number of cards in a deck, nor the number of strings on a fiddle, nor danced a step in my life. If I had blighted the innocency of my infancy, the buoyancy of my boyhood, the vigor of my youth, and the enterprise of my young manhood, with serving the devil, God would never have blessed me with this superabounding labor.

Recently I went back to my native land, after a period of twenty-seven years having elapsed since I was presiding elder in that country. I preached under a sugar tree, which I had planted with my own hand when a little boy. It afforded shade enough for five hundred people. I looked in vain for my schoolmates and saw not one. I heard of some in other countries whither they had emigrated. What was the solution? "The wicked shall not live out half their days." Upon inquiry, calling them by name, I was notified that they were in their graves; though they were physical stalwarts, promising long life, and myself comparatively and notoriously the dwarf of the neighborhood, yet doing more work even in my little boyhood than those stalwarts. I am so glad I said "yes" to the Holy Ghost in my infancy and have perpetuated that "yea and amen" through this fleeting life, which will soon be o'er, as

now I am almost eighty-two, and looking on the last
mile-post, electrified with the shouts of the angels
beyond the last river; constantly looking for His
glorious appearing to transfigure this frail and fleeting body, or an angel whom, in case He tarrieth, He
will soon send, as He did for Lazarus, to call me
to evacuate it, to rest a little while on the bosom of
terra firma and fly away to join the loved ones gone
on before, and now awaiting me on the bright, shining shore.

> "Oh! 'tis sweet to think hereafter,
> When the spirit leaves this sphere,
> Love with deathless wings, shall waft her
> To those she long hath mourned for here,
> Hearts from which 'twas death to sever,
> Eyes this world can ne'er restore,
> There as warm and bright as ever,
> Will greet us and be lost no more."

In infancy the Holy Ghost comes and puts His
loving hand on you, taking you in His hands like
Jesus did the children in all His peregrinations on
earth. That is the reason why babies always mani-
fest a loving disposition, being ready to go to any
body, like their beautiful symbol, the lamb, which
goes to the dog as readily as to its own mother.
Now suppose the infant is not encouraged by its
parents, who, to our sorrow and the grief of the
Holy Spirit, are, in the great majority, shamefully
ignorant of the relation of the little ones to the
Kingdom. Consequently they have no idea that they
can be intelligently converted to God and started
on the heavenly way, as that hereditary depravity
in every one turns the face away from God, toward

the wicked world. If not converted, *i. e.*, turned round and introduced to God, it will go right away into sin, thus forfeiting its justification and, like the prodigal son, becoming a backslider. Thus, when the Holy Ghost invites the little one to come to Jesus, as He wants to give him a happy introduction, and thus start him out on the heavenly way, he says, "I am too little to get religion; mamma says I must wait till I get to be a big boy and know what I am doing."

Then the Holy Spirit, thus treated with contempt by the little child, whom He so much wanted to win for Jesus, before the devil ever got his black hand on him, goes away, grieved and unappreciated. He remembers the promise the child made to receive Him when he became a large boy. Therefore, taking him at his word, He comes to the stalwart lad, but does not take him in His arms as when an infant, because he has already gotten away from the Lord, and yielded to Satan's temptations, contracting wicked habits, and becoming a poor backslider. Consequently the Holy Spirit stops in ten paces and calls him, "Son, give me thine heart. Those who seek me early shall find me. Come now, let us go up to the house of the Lord." He has gone wild and fallen in with wicked company, therefore he says, "Lord, I am too young, let me wait till I get to be a grown man and I will seek the Lord with all my might and make sure of Heaven." Thus he has again hardened his heart, stiffened his neck and rejected the Holy Ghost, treating with contempt His merciful overtures.

The years speed their precipitate flight, boyhood, striplinghood and youth have flown away, he is now a full-grown young man, the time having arrived when he had promised the Holy Spirit to receive Him and seek the Lord. Taking him at his word, He comes again, not into his immediate presence, as in infancy, nor in nice speaking distance, ten steps, as when he was a growing lad, but He stands off a hundred yards and lifts up His loving, heavenly voice, "Rejoice, O young man, in thy youth. Let thy heart cheer thee; in the days of thy youth, walk in the ways of thine heart and in the sight of thine eyes, but know thou, that for all these things God will bring thee into judgment." This, you see, is irony, like the mother would say to her child, "Go ahead with your disobedience, but I have the hickory for you, and will give you plenty of it in due time." But he responds, "Lord, I am so tied up with juvenile societies and organizations, which I cannot abandon now, I must enjoy the pleasures of the world a little while, I just can't get away from my associates to become a Christian now, please excuse me till I reach mature manhood, and I'll leave all my wicked companions forever, seek and serve the Lord with all my heart, for I must get to Heaven when I die."

Satan's policy is indefinite postponement. "While the lamp holds out to burn, the vilest sinner may return." That is so, he *may* return, but only one in a million *does;* hence, over that poetry-greased plank he slides the giddy multitudes into the bottomless pit. The blessed Holy Spirit is thus grieved and treated with contempt, because God's time is *now*, as He says, "Now is the accepted time; now is the day of salvation; if ye hear his voice, harden not your heart."

True to this young man's promise, that he will give the Lord his heart when he has reached mature manhood, the Holy Spirit comes again, but not into his immediate presence, as when in infantile justification; nor in boyhood, when He came in ten steps and appealed to him with all the fervency of a loving father; nor in his youth, when He halted a hundred yards from 'him and lifted up His stentorian voice, and preached the Gospel with the pathos of Judgment-day honesty; but now He is still farther off and, lifting up His stentorian voice, He administers the solemn warning, "Lay not up for yourselves treasures where moth and rust corrupt and thieves break through and steal. But lay up for yourselves treasure in heaven, where neither moth nor rust corrupt, nor thieves break through nor steal. For where your treasure is, there will your heart be also."

By this time the man is running at locomotive speed after filthy lucre; having been caught by Mammon's wild lasso, going for everything, where he can find a dollar! He is hot after monopolies and trusts, hallucinated with the glowing conception of the millionaire. The deceitfulness of riches has actually so manipulated him with its paralyzing hand as to eclipse the glorious Sun of Righteousness, so that

not a solitary ray reaches his soul. Really he is
blind to what does not glisten and deaf to what does
not jingle, and a devout worshiper at the shrine of
Eureka. Therefore he responds, "Lord, You must
excuse me. I am so encumbered that I cannot possi-
bly give any attention to religion! I will have to
wait till I make a living and can thus disencumber
myself; I trow by that time life's evening will be
creeping on and I will go out of business and have
nothing to do but seek the Lord, give my attention
to the salvation of my soul, spend life's evening in
His service, and be ripe and ready for a glorious
immortality when this fleeting life is over."

Thus the blessed Holy Spirit is again disappointed, rejected, and His loving mercy treated with contempt. Therefore He takes the man at his word,
goes away and returns no more until his gray locks
fall over his corrugated temples and his hoary head
is thus blooming for the tomb. Then the blessed
Holy Spirit gives him another call, but does not
come nigh, as in infancy, when He took him in His
arms; and in childhood, when He came in ten steps;
and in youth, when He came in a hundred yards;
and in manhood, when He came within a furlong;
but now he calls from a distant hilltop: "Turn ye,
Oh, turn ye, for why will ye die? As I live, saith
the Lord, I have no pleasure in the death of the
wicked, but that he turn from his evil way and live.
Turn ye, oh, turn ye, for why will ye die?"

By this time the poor man has become skeptical.
His ear is dull, so he but faintly hears the call of

the Holy Ghost; his eyes so dim that his recognition
is like the *ignis fatuus,* whose delusive ray lights
up unreal worlds and glows but to betray. He has
passed over the summit and is going down, to return no more, and soon drops dead with heart
failure.

Thus with prolixity I have answered the question
often raised, "What is the unpardonable sin
and how committed?" As Jesus says, it is the blasphemy of the Spirit, treating the Holy Ghost with
contempt, finally rejecting Him. As a rule, it is
done periodically and epochally. Thus inadvertently
as life gets away, before we are aware the last moment has fled and we are out in eternity, never to
regain probationary opportunity. While, as a rule
it supervenes, gradually and progressively, without
the slightest anticipation of the awful coming damnation, yet it does not always come that way. Some-
times in the bloom of youth a person so rebuffs the
Holy Spirit with blasphemous contempt that God
says of him, "Let him alone, let him believe a lie
and be damned." In many instances people sin so
outrageously as to alienate the Holy Spirit forever,
crossing the fatal line, and sinning away the fatal
time, and sealing their doom in Hell.

> "There is a line by man unseen,
>   Which crosses every path,
> The hidden boundary between
>   God's mercy and His wrath.
> "There is a time,
>   We know not when,
> A point, we know not where,
>   Which marks the destiny of men to glory or despair."

If you sin away the auspicious time and cross the fatal line, you are eternally doomed. Therefore the thing to do is to say "yes" to the Holy Ghost at every cost, leaving the devil, world without end, giving him back everything you ever got from him, which is all your sins, and dash off up the King's highway of holiness, which Jesus has built with His own bleeding, toiling hands, every inch from the city of destruction to the New Jerusalem. No lion nor ravenous beast, nor toll gate on it; perfectly free for all, regardless of race, color, social station, or nationality. Thus, with ever accelerated velocity, sweep on without a backward glance, till you reach the Pearly Portals, leap through the gate with a shout of victory, and receive a crown of glory that will never fade away, but accumulate new luster through the flight of eternal ages.

When Julius Cæsar conquered the Gauls and Britain, i. e., France and England, two thousand years ago, he always made it a rule to burn down all the bridges, so retreat was impossible; they had to conquer those bloodthirsty barbarians or be cut all to pieces. There was really nothing before them but victory or death. The result was, he took those countries by conquest. This is the thing for every human soul to do, leave the devil now and burn down all the bridges as you cross out of his kingdom, so you never can get back.

CHAPTER IV.

Satan is the great counterfeiter and invariably counterfeits everything that God does.

"Hypocrite" is a Greek word and means, originally, an actor on the theatrical stage, performing an unreal part.

When Jesus was on earth He scathed and peeled the scribes and Pharisees from top to toe, denouncing them as hypocrites who would not escape the damnation of Hell; whereas they were the honored and dignified clergy, pastors of the churches and the office-bearers of the theocracy. Many think our Savior was a most unpopular preacher. He was with the officials of church and state, because they knew that His success meant their dethronement; whereas with the people He was the most popular preacher the world ever saw.

Although He made no appointments, the very earth trembled beneath the thronging multitudes everywhere accompanying Him, hanging with breathless silence upon His eloquent lips; even so enthused with His preaching and His mighty works that they would not go away to eat, but stayed day after day, out in the desert, physically famishing, so that He miraculously fed them with loaves and fishes, ten

28

thousand people feasting on only food enough for five, even though all had taken a Benjamin's mess, as their long fast had given them voracious appetites. Finally at the conclusion, the fragmentary edibles surviving were about a hundred times the original quantity.

The officials got so mad at Him for exposing their transparent hypocrisy that they actually manipulated the Roman authorities to arrest Him on the false accusation of high treason. This they had to do in the night, and they would have crucified Him before day, if they could have gotten Pilate out of his downy bed to sit on the case and sign His death warrant. They had been thirsting for His blood three years, and would have killed Him, if they had not feared the people, who always heard Him gladly. If the people had known what was going on, they would have rallied, fought, bled and died for Him. If Pilate, who knew He was innocent, had been amply supplied with soldiers, he would not have crucified Him, but have protected Him.

Thus hypocrisy is playing religion, *i. e.,* professing and not possessing. May the Holy Spirit so illuminate your minds that you will wake up to the fact that the world is this day full of Satan's counterfeit religion, professing instead of possessing; hypocrisy instead of the glorious reality.

Oh, how all Hell is now laden under embargo to counterfeit everything God does. How climacteric the case which forms the subject of this booklet; the anti-paraclete, who not only denies the Holy Ghost, but has the audacity to take His place and claim to be the Comforter. I verily believe that any person who will aspire to it, can have a following in our day.

It seems that the very witticism of Hell is focalized now to find sidetracks on which to run out from the great trunk line leading to the New Jerusalem. Satan manipulates most adroitly, laying down the sidetracks so parallel with the main trunk that the passenger, especially if he is taking a nap, utterly fails to recognize it. It is so parallel at the beginning that, without special notification, none of us would find out that we have left the New Jerusalem trunk line. It gradually deflects more and more, till finally it superinduces a complete sommersault, running directly back whence you came; so the passengers are in full anticipation of the Celestial City till they actually arrive and look out for angel bands and beloved saints gone on before, to meet them on the bright, shining shore, but utterly disappointed as of course no one comes to meet them.

When Bunyan's Pilgrim was on his way to the Celestial City, he met that well-dressed man, Ignorance, with whom he had conversed when he came up that crooked, grassy lane to the King's Highway and put his foot on it and traveled deliberately like other pilgrims; Christian interviewing him discovered he had not come through that little narrow wicket gate, at the head of the highway, to whom he responded that the people in his country had a nigh way to cut across and escape all the troubles encountered in passing the gate, and also that awful quagmire, the

Slough of Despond, and other places where they had
giants and demons to fight.

Finally, when Christian and Hopeful reached the
flooded Jordan, they crossed with much peril and
difficulty, Christian sinking under the flood three
times, as it was so deep he could not reach the
bottom with his feet and would have gone down
if Hopeful had not held him up. When he reached
the other shore angel bands met him and escorted
him up Mt. Zion to the City of God, where he knock-
ed at the gate and the patriarchs and prophets
asked him for his certificate, *i. e.*, the witness of the
Spirit, which he had carried all along his pilgrimage,
with the little exception of when he ventured to take
a nap in the delightful arbor beside the way as they
climbed Mt. Difficulty, where he lost it and had to
go back, and fortunately found it.

When the patriarchs and prophets demanded
it, he had it all right and presented it to them, when
the gate opened wide and he entered with shouts
of victory.

Looking back over the jasper walls, he sees Ignorance arrive at the flooded Jordan, who beckoned
to old Vain Hope, who kept a ferry there and moved
it up for his accommodation, so he got aboard and
crossed the swelling flood without difficulty. Reaching the shore down at the base of great Mt. Zion,
no angel bands met him, but he thought nothing of
it, but walked deliberately and with dignity up the
mountain with staff in hand. Reaching the Celestial
Gate, he knocks with his staff deliberately, still un-

suspicious of trouble. The patriarchs and prophets look over and demand his certificate, but he was speechless. Then the tormentors from Hell come right to the gate of Heaven, take possession of him and carry him a nigh way, right through to the bottomless pit.

It is high time that all sincere people get their eyes open to the awful heresies which are afloat in the air beneath every sky; "cunningly devised fables," of which we are warned in the Pauline prophecies. My library of paper-bound books, every one on a different subject, not only expounds every grand truth revealed in the Bible, and essential to salvation, but exposes the diversified heresies hatched in Hell, and propagated by Satan's preachers throughout the world. Among those booklets we have "God's Triple Leadership," which should be in the hands of every person. Man is a trinity, consisting of spirit, soul and body; the Holy Spirit leads the human spirit; the Word, the intelligent; and providence, the body. If you are true to this triple leadership, which is simple and easily understood, you will never go wrong. God says, "My people perish for lack of knowledge." That does not mean that Satan's people go down to Hell, but God's own people perish for lack of knowledge. Hence we should all do our best to spread the knowledge of God's blessed, saving truth throughout the whole world, as it is the only antidote aainst Satan's false teachings, which his preachers are now carrying to the ends of the earth.

www.ingramcontent.com/pod-product-compliance
Lightning Source LLC
Chambersburg PA
CBHW030312030426
42337CB00012B/689